Pen and Inks

Lisa Talbott

Illustrations by Lucas Volaart-Vermeulen

Illustrations by Lucas Volaart-Vermeulen

AuthorHouse™ UK
1663 Liberty Drive
Bloomington, IN 47403 USA
www.authorhouse.co.uk
Phone: 0800 047 8203 (Domestic TFN)
+44 1908 723714 (International)

This book is printed on acid-free paper.

ISBN: 978-1-7283-9439-8 (sc)
ISBN: 978-1-7283-9438-1 (e)

Print information available on the last page.

Published by AuthorHouse 11/26/2019

authorHOUSE®

"I'm fat, so what?"

My husband's such a lucky man.
Lucky he's not dead!
He 'dared' to call me FAT, last week
. . . hence he's sleeping in the shed.

I admit, those words were stinging.
He cut me to the quick!
I sulked for hours: I planned revenge.
He'll eat his words. The dick.

Then I studied my reflection.
It hurts, you know; plain truth.
Hey I'm 63 for goodness sake,
no longer in my youth.

But I suppose a little exercise,
wouldn't be amiss.
I'll join a gym, to humour him,
my arse he'll have to kiss.

Well, I managed seven press-ups,
then I stopped to have a cig.
I started running on the spot,
. . sweating like a pig.

Round the block I tried to jog,
sporting my new Nikes
My next-door neighbour's four year olds
passed me on their trikes!

I came back ruddy shackered!
My t-shirt soaking wet.
Not sure I like this fitness lark.
Lipo's MY best bet.

A whole darn week I struggled.
I lost a pound. Big deal.
I hate those models in the mags,
(at least my boobs are real!)

So stuff the diet, embrace my curves,
and stuff his words! How vicious?!
The dog still loves me - fat or thin,
. . ooh this cream cake's damn delicious

1

"Revenge"

Whole dark thoughts surround me as I calm my shaking hand.
And hoping, once my deed is done, perhaps you'll understand?
There ARE no second chances now, you waived them all away,
confident in knowing you'll succeed another day.

So tired of all your cheating. Your lies; your cruel deceit.
I've found my strength to end this now: It's going to be my treat.
I thought I'd try to stab you, but I loathe the sight of blood,
and burning down your house would only scare the neighbourhood.

But ARSENIC is a great idea, concealed in Shepherd's Pie!
Revenge is such a sweet duress. A classic 'eye-for-eye'!
I'll try to kill you quickly, though your suff'ring would be swell!
an' I'll have to move the body quick before you start to smell

I mixed the poison slowly which I added to the beef.
"Prepare to meet thy Master!" . . Whilst I rehearse my grief.
You won't suspect a thing because although I'm filled with dread,
I'll lead you to assume a night of passion lies ahead.

Well, the morning dawned as normal and I'm shaking like a leaf,
he's still alive and kicking, and I stare in disbelief.
I cursed my foolish efforts, thinking "why is he not dead"!?
So I checked again the label! Duh! - I'd bought ARNICA instead !!

"Vegas Bombshell"

I gazed at this band on my finger.
It shone in the dark of the night.
And I turned to a man snoring loudly,
whom just hours, I'd pledged Mr Right.

I reflected my journey to be here.
The flirts, and the laughs, and the games.
We were carried away on the height of the day
and I'm damned if I remember his name!

I flew out to Vegas this August,
'cos I needed some sun and some sex.
I'd submitted my notice at Aldi
and bid 'adieus' to my ex!

Well Vegas was truly amazing.
I'd left all my shackles behind.
I met Elvis, . . and Elvis, . . and Elvis.
And everyone seems really kind!

I dabbled a bit on the tables,
whilst sporting my finest fake jewels.
I lost quite a bit the first evening;
but slowly caught on to the rules.

I winked, and I blinked, and I pouted.
And I guzzled champagne, all night long.
Then I won short of two million dollars!!
And whoooosh I was no longer alone!

Oh the staff couldn't have been any kinder!
I was given the best luxury suite!
They brought Anna to make me look younger,
and Rico to massage my feet

Rico and I got 'acquainted' . . .
(Wouldn't you, just adore a masseur?)
I giggled like a born-again schoolgirl.
(I had parts never massaged before!)

The next several hours are all blurry.
Hence this hunk in his bronzed 'birthday suit'.
I panicked! I want a good lawyer,
to perform a decree absolute!

But the champagne continued next morning.
And Rico? Still keen to perform
I dismissed every thought of a lawyer . .
damn it all, any port in a storm!

"In memory of . . ."

I dreamt of you last night, my love.
It all felt truly grand.
We were walking on a beach somewhere;
barefoot in the sand.

You told me how you'd missed me.
I said I'd missed you too.
You apologised for leaving
but there was nothing you could do.

You told me you were "happy now"
and that I was not to grieve.
And you couldn't stay much longer here
'cos again you'll have to leave.

You turned me round to face you.
We hugged, and then we kissed.
That taste of you! The smell of you . .
everything I've missed.

We walked along that empty beach
holding hands, I sobbed.
Mindful of those years we loved,
and of a future we were robbed.

You asked if we were wrong back then, and if we had our chance again,
"Would we . . if we could"?
I laughed out loud, threw back my head,
"In a heartbeat. Yes, I would."

"Girls night in"

We're all much too old for the nightclubs these days, so instead, we have 'girlie nights in'.
We no longer go clubbin' where the music's just thumpin' cos at our age it's classed as a sin!

Going out isn't even 'our thing' nowadays, think we'd faint at the prices of booze!
With most of us married, late nights leave us harried . . preferring an afternoon snooze.

It's a Rule that we all bring a bottle (or two) and we'll polish off easy, the lot.
By the end of the night it's one hell of a fright, with most of us losing the plot.

So Thursday, the night was Rebecca's to host, and the entourage gathered en mass.
T'was also a birthday of one of us thirty so she'd balloons filled with hydrogen gas!?!?!?

Rebecca made curry, lasagne, and chilli, she always cooks loads for us girls.
The table looked great, garlic bread set on plates, for desert there were Viennese Whirls.

Conversation was growing, the vodka was flowing then Jenny untied a red a ballon.
She held up her light, and she tried to ignite . . then whoooosh! There was SUCH a loud boom!

"Rebecca you ass, you pur-chased the wrong gas, it was helium you needed to buy"!
The kitchen got torched, all our eyebrows got scorched, and we thought we were all gonna die!

With the hydrogen leaking, the flames hit the ceiling, then somebody called 999.
We tried sobering up as the flames overtook and all fled . . with our glasses of wine!

'Course her husband went spare, (thank god we weren't there) but the insurers were great, and paid up.
But our partners demanded our girls nights' disbanded, and insist we now meet in the pub!

"The girl at the station"

She sat there with her suitcase,
I watched her from the bar.
She was scanning, searching, waiting . .
Her demeanour quite bizarre.

She looked a slight bedraggled.
Anxious; almost manic.
She checked her watch a hundred times.
She bore that stance of panic.

15? 16? Not much more.
A beauty, there's no doubt.
I watched a half hour longer.
Today is MY 'stake-out'.

A woman came to greet her.
Some tough guy by her side.
The 'girl at the station' beamed a smile.
Relief, she couldn't hide.

I smiled an' relaxed with my coffee.
It's fun to 'people watch'.
But I had this deep sick feeling
when the guy grabbed hold her crotch!

The 'girl at the station' withered.
Her smile disappeared, she withdrew.
I watched from the bar, in confusion??
But knew all at once, what to do.

I called 999 from my mobile,
relaying the details I had.
I walked to the 'girl at the station'
and showed Mr Nasty my badge!

Nadia came from Lithuania.
She'd been promised a job doing nails,
(Her family had coughed up a fortune.)
belying the sordid details.

The girl at the station's not here now.
She studied and got a degree;
in Lithuania exploiting sex traffickers.
And sponsored entirely by me.

"Why I'm divorcing my husband"

I'm getting divorced from my husband,
and I'm filing the papers forthwith.
I hate him with such a great passion.
He doesn't deserve to let live.

The arsehole is well in his sixties,
his youth and his sex appeal - gone.
So I told him we needed some romance
or I'd leave him before very long.

We've always been different in lifestyle.
I'm a firm Naturalist you see.
I love Science, and nature, and animals.
He just likes beer and TV.

After weeks of 'unsubtle' persuasion
he finally agreed to concede;
So he booked us a caravan in Brighton,
to rekindle 'just what we need'

Bless him, he sorted out everything.
What a great week this will be!
I dismissed all the negatives between us,
just so thrilled that he did this for me.

I donned my new shorts and my sunhat
and admit that I looked pretty Chic.
I jogged to the beach to locate him.
And THAT'S when I hated the dick!

I recoiled in my tracks in pure horror!
The fool booked a NATURIST Park!
I hid at the back of a boulder,
praying it soon would be dark.

Everyone's running round naked!
Playing tennis, or rounders - no less!
All that flesh, not a blush, what a nightmare!
'cos I was the only one dressed!

And of course!! There on the beach - my 'beloved' ??
Taking pics, with his old Brownie Box!
Clearly enjoying the scenery . .
and starkers! Apart from his socks!

"Communiquè"

I was smiling whilst shopping this morning,
said "good morning" to folk in the queue.
They stared at me like I'm a nutter,
and didn't know quite what to do!

See, people don't TALK to each other.
Strangers don't like your approach.
Everyone's 'cool' and elusive.
Their space you should never encroach.

NO-ONE is calling our house phone,
and we're paying a hefty month's fee!
But with FaceTime, 'n WhatsApp, 'n Messenger,
you can call the whole world now for free!

You don't even need to go shopping.
Your phone is an 'internet Store'
You search it, you find it, you buy it.
It's delivered next day to your door.

When I want any update on family,
I'll find it on Facebook, for sure.
I'll know if they're dead, wed, or otherwise,
'cos no-one sends cards any more.

See, as children we'd CALL for each other!
We knocked on friends' doors, all en-mass.
Great gath'rings of children conversing.
Their heads all now bent, tapping glass.

Pencils and pens once wrote letters.
Now that's all a thing of the past.
The digital future accelerating.
Conversation is history, alas.

Oh to go back to those old days,
when our phones only rang in our hall.
And who can remember red kiosks?
Where fourpence would buy you a call.

When I'm dead and my iPad's redundant,
when I CAN'T write, or phone just to talk,
nor ABLE to text or send emails,
I'll just 'chat' on the old Ouija Board!

10

"Praying for rain"

I wish it would ruddy well rain. Today I got sunburnt again!
The temperature's soaring, t'was 40 this morning; It's driving me flippin' insane!

I tried taking shade by the trees, but they're literally teeming with bees,
I was recently stung at the base of my bum. Oh I wish it was fifteen degrees.

I burned and I blistered, then peeled. My back's full of scabs, all congealed
See, the wind can be fooling, when blowing and cooling, I should've applied a sun shield.

And you CANNOT eat anything hot. Barbecues? definitely not!
I've a scar way up high, from a hot chicken thigh . . (I could show you, but p'haps better not.)

Aw, the sun's been a scorcher for weeks, giving me wrinkles all over me cheeks!
It's aged me this year, showing perfectly clear that I'm needing some miracle creams.

So before I start sunning again, I'll slap on at least Factor 10,
'Cos my pals there in Blighty, would swear I was ninety. (No chance of me 'pulling' young men).

Yay!! It rained and ye God's did it pour! Eight sandbags outside the front door.
The pool's full of shite, and the garden's a fright, Ooh I wish it was hot, like before

"The Whitwick 35"

John Albert Gee was just thirteen
when he worked down the mine.
John Albert Gee. That tragedy!
"The Whitwick 35".

April 1898.
A village struck by grief.
An eerie silence borne to those
in shock, and disbelief.

The fire raged as lives were claimed
of husbands, brothers, sons.
Whilst frantic families, in despair,
prayed for their loved ones.

The price of coal; too high a goal.
Too many lives were lost.
And mining towns the whole world wide
have paid the same high cost.

John Albert Gee will always be
a boy, of no more years.
No life to live, no sin to forgive,
still wet behind the ears.

Remember 1898.
Remember all those men.
Don't let them be forgotten.
Let's honour them again.

"The cake thief"

I adore the wild nightlife in London.
For me, it's a time to feel good.
The bars and the nightclubs are beckoning;
where it's easy to pull a young stud.

I spend days sorting out what I'm wearing.
The make-up, the undies, the hair.
Competition in London's tremendous;
(and nobody knows me down there).

First Class, is the way that I travel,
and I start as I mean to go on.
Travel Lodges are out of the question!
The Ritz being MY number one!

I preempted my dealer beforehand.
Needing Charlie, amphetamines, and 'coke'.
I withdrew a few monkeys beforehand,
(cash only, for this kinda bloke!)

Oh, the weekend was truly stupendous.
(Though my memory's not totally clear!)
But I must've coerced a good deal then,
'cos hey! I'm surrounded by gear!

I've got weed, I've got smack, I've got powders.
I've got ice and I've even got cake!
I could sell the whole lot down my local!
A ruddy great fortune I'd make!

I returned to my dwelling, hungover.
Flaked out, fell asleep on my bed.
I'd dumped all my stash in the kitchen,
to attend in the morning instead.

But my mother called round in the morning.
Made coffee, and ate all my cake!
I found her spaced out in the armchair.
Eyes glazing, as if wide awake!

I've changed all the locks in my house now.
I daren't have my mum just drop round.
And the truth is, I can't ever tell her,
she's the oldest drug user in town!

"The day I went for my smear test"

I received a short note from my doctor,
to inform me my smear test is due.
It's a ritual us ladies don't relish,
but a necessary thing we all do.

My appointment was for 6, on the Friday,
so I'd needed to go straight from work.
No chance to rush home for a shower;
the time disallowing this perk.

On arrival, I nipped to 'The Ladies',
to apply a quick 'spit and a wipe'
with a tissue I found in my handbag,
'cos no-one likes being thought 'ripe'

I nervously sat till they called me.
It's a man! This is horribly wrong!
Why didn't I go for a waxing?!?
And why did I wear this damn thong?

"Draw your knees to your bottom, then drop 'em"!
Tis SUCH an undignified pose!
My blush carried right past my bosom.
But he's used to it all, I suppose?

The instrument looked pretty archaic!
Anxiety caused my heart beat to race!
Out of nowhere, and quite uncontrollably !!!
I broke wind right in front of his face!

But no folks; my shame didn't end there.
I fled, trying hard not to linger!
But Doc calls me back from Reception,
waving my thong round his finger!

"Mother Nature is a bitch"

I've got creams, I've got lotions and potions.
I've got tablets and powders and pills.
I've got aches, I've got pains, and I've problems . .
now I'm as 'old as the hills'.

I've got leaks, I've got squeaks, and a bunion.
I'm hating this battle with age.
I've got callouses, gout, and rheumatics.
My ailments could fill a whole page!

I've dentures, n' glasses, a zimmer!
A Pacemaker's next on the list.
You may think I'm 'eggs-aggerating',
believe me there's not much I've missed.

The internet proves that I'm dying.
I've researched all my troubles on line.
I'm no longer as 'fit as fiddle',
but it helps when I have a good whine. (Or a good wine)

I eat veggies and fruits, (but no meat now)
and anything fresh from the sea.
I partake in a large glass of Merlot,
(for longevity reasons you see!)

I buy clothes that are comfy and baggy.
And I've girdles to 'hold me all in'.
The stuff I've donated to Oxfam!
'cos sadly I'm no longer thin!

I cancelled the keep-fit and yoga.
I struggle to climb in the bath!
And I've slung all the mirrors in our house.
Mother Nature is having a laugh.

Yes, the future looks grim for us old 'uns,
as our consciences err to defiance.
So I'm donating my wealth to the Cats' Home.
and my body to medical science.

"I love Alex Randall. By Ellie, aged 6"

I luv Alex Randall.
His in my class at school.
Mum sez he went to heaven.
I think heaven's cool.

He's always really funny.
He has the class in bits.
He'd breakdance in our classroom.
"Please Miss. What is 'fits'?"

My uncle Carl dint like him.
He said he weren't no good.
(Carl's not my REAL uncle,
but mom's a widowhood).

Uncle Carl is horrid.
He drinks, and then he's rude!
He walks without his clothes on
an' his body's all tattooed.

(He calls me his sweet princess
But I'm not, I wear no crown!
And he hurts me; I don't like it
when my mom is not around).

The last time I saw Alex
was about sicks weeks ago:
down the park behind the pub
where Uncle Carl would go.

Well . . we were really laffin
cos we thought we heard some pigs!
Grunting really loudly . .
then Alex stood on twigs!

The pigs then stopped their grunting.
And evryfink went wrong,
cos the 'pigs' appeared before us . .
Carl, but not my mom!!

He screamed at me 'n Alex
"Tell, and yore both dead"
Then Alex, started twitching.
I ran home instead.

I was gonna tell my mom
but she was playin' on her fone.
Then there's Alex on the tele!
People beggin' he come home?

Uncle Carl is now in prizun.
I am glad he's gone away.
"Mom! PLEEEEZ let's go heaven.
I miss my friend today".

"Social media, woohoo!"

Facebook is a brilliant tool for folk to keep in touch.
Twitter, Skype and WhatsApp, (though don't care for them that much).
To find old mates, and old flames too just seek and ye shall find!
But be careful what you wish for, cos the internet's a Mine!

I tried to find an ex of mine from years and years ago.
Oh he was cool! A demi-god! I sadly let him go.
So searched his name; behold! he's here! I'll message straight away!
. . . We're meeting up next Tuesday, and I'm buzzing for that day.

I need to sort my wardrobe, cos I don't know what to wear!
I've bought a brand new lipstick, and a colour for my hair.
I got a panti-girdle, which it claims will 'hold me in'!
Remember, this guy knows me from the days when I was thin.

I got some strong adhesive too, these dentures make me gag!
The Tweed cologne I used to wear will surely drive him mad.
We'll reminisce, perhaps we'll kiss? Please pray it all goes well?
Will let you all know after, (cos I love to 'kiss and tell')

. . . . .

Well, I don't know how to say this cos I'm bloody boiling mad!
I told you he was gorgeous and a right 'Sir Galahad'.
I filled a Pools form out in '84 and damn! I left it there.
I won! He claimed. Now HE'S a millionaire!

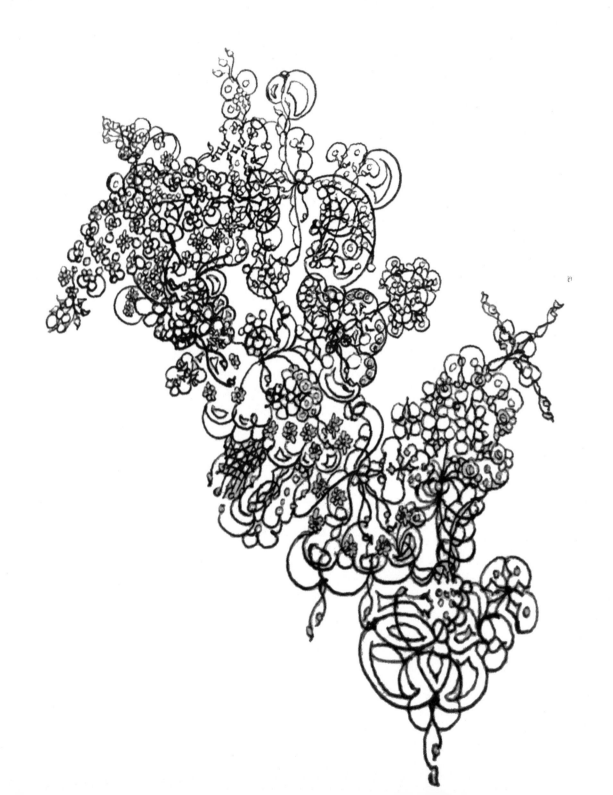

"The invisible pain"

The pain of grief is manifold.
A pain one cannot see.
Indescribable by words.
And can happen instantly.

A wound can heal.
A limb can mend.
But a heart can ache
for years on end.

The pain of grief's a personal thing.
Only time, 'they' say, can heal.
It's measured how? In weeks or years?
How do 'they' know how you'll feel?

It's an open sore.
Never goes away.
Every song, every smell
brings a memory.

The pain of grief is a blessed thing.
It means you've loved; but lost.
And only those who're hurting most,
will forever count the cost.

"The boy next door"

Lee and I were neighbours.
So I guess I knew him well.
Far kinder than my brothers.
Compassionate as well.

His family were all instrumental.
(And I mean in the musical vein.)
He spent hours perfecting his ivories . .
over and over again.

Our schooldays weren't a pleasure.
(Remember! Lee's my mate.)
His feminine side was offensive,
to the bully-boys, armed with hate.

But Lee was ultra ambitious.
He conjectured fame: and more.
I was filled with admiration,
for the 'boy who lived next door'.

He created an Adonis-like image.
He yearned for the big Silver Screens.
And he got it . . . cos he earned it!
Revered in the top magazines.

His shows! Extravaganza!
Performed to the créme de la créme
The jibes and taunts of his schooldays
never caused anguish again.

He EPITOMISED "flamboyant".
Sporting furs, and jewels, and wealth.
But his lifestyle (though once so private)
mocked him in bad health.

To his kinfolk - he was WALTER.
To his friends - he was always LEE.
To the world, my friend and neighbour . .
"THE SHOWMAN - LIBERACE"

"Forgotten"

The old boy lay huddled in the doorway.
his slippers were old, and well-worn.
His trousers were ragged and dirty.
His shirt - all tattered and torn.

He looked so unkempt and so still there.
His hair and his beard, too long.
An aura of sadness surrounds him.
A soul with a story gone wrong.

His bed was made up of old boxes,
no warmth could they ever provide.
An old basket to house his possessions:
A whimpering black dog by his side.

Did you know that he once was a hero?
Did you know he was once young and brave?
Did you know that he fought with his comrades?
But his dignity, no-one could save.

His medals, he kept in his pocket.
No family to extol of his past.
No friends to meet up for a pint with.
His life has been hardly a blast!

Sirens shriek out their arrival.
It's time for this old boy to leave.
His faithful black dog's all alone now.
. . the only soul living to grieve.

"Goodbye sweet love?"

Hug me while I cry a little.
Calm me whilst I sob.
Hold my hand a moment more,
you'll have finished then, your job.

Walk away, and don't look back.
And please - don't slam the door.
Take your heart to your new love
and pity me no more.

All the signs I failed to see.
Because of course, love's blind.
But your parting words will ever haunt
this girl, you leave behind.

I'll think of you when I drink tea.
I'll reach for you at night.
I'll speak your name a thousand times;
but don't doubt I'll be alright.

I know I should wish you happiness.
I know I should wish you well.
But the worm has turned, 'cos this bitch was spurned,
and I hope that you rot in Hell!

"I'm sorry"

What did I do wrong today to make you leave me here?
I tried to run to catch you but my cries you couldn't hear.

I thought it must've been a game but dad, you left no food!
So I must've been a naughty boy to put you in this mood.

I'm sorry if I barked a lot, I'm sad when all alone.
You know I'm at my happiest when everyone's at home.

I'm sorry too for all that mess; I knew you'd both complain,
but I couldn't get to go outside, my hip's in too much pain.

Remember all the pics you took when I was just a pup?
And how I cried for days because I missed my mum so much?

But you and mum and me and cat we made our lives just great.
You took me on exciting hikes, told all I'm YOUR best mate.

Those shoes I chewed six years ago; don't tell me you're still mad?
Of course I chase the cat around, s'a game that we both had.

That little baby girl last week, that grew in mummy's tum?
I hoped that she and me were gonna grow to have such fun!

It's getting really late and I'm so scared in this dark place.
Oh please come soon to fetch me back, I need to lick your face.

Forgive me please for all my wrongs: Just learn to count to ten.
Now turn around and take me home, and love me once again.

"My secret"

I have a little secret which I'm gonna let you know!
I hid my Will in a biscuit tin, many moons ago.
I also wrote a little note and tucked it safe inside.
Some photos too, of my bygone years; to be opened when I died.

That biscuit tin's well hidden and I'm SURE it's full of rust,
I never told a single soul, for there's no one I would trust.
A fortune from my lifetime? Bequeathed to all those left?
Can my legacy bring them joy, or will they feel bereft?

Would love to see their faces when they get this gift from me
Can see them booking flights to destinations 'cross the sea.
Champagne corks a-popping as they work out what to buy.
And I feel a little guilty, as I deem to tell you why.

I've spent the ruddy lot you see, and I have had a ball!
No old timer's home for me, the beer-off's had it all
Not a dime, nor a pound; there is nothing that they're due,
There's just THAT piece of paper. A simple I.O.U.!

"Why I don't shop in Lidl anymore"

I saw this guy in Lidl,
bagging up some leeks.
He was truly 'drop dead gorgeous'!
A blush grew on my cheeks.

I followed with my trolley,
he looked like Dwayne, The Rock.
Course, I didn't know his real name,
so called him "three o'clock".

At 3.00 p.m. each Friday,
to Lidl I would go.
Dressed up in my 'Sunday best'
hoping he would show.

Went overboard with perfume,
I sprayed Chanel Allure.
I wore my bright red lippie.
He's worth it. J't'adore!

My luck was struck last Friday!
This 'vision' in the aisle.
We chatted over trollies.
I gave my Hollywood smile.

I giggled like a schoolgirl,
flirting like a fool.
And then his partner joined us,
I then became 'Miss Cool'.

His partner too, was stunning.
They both wore wedding bands.
They wed in San Francisco.
His partner's name is Hans!

"My weaks and daze of a dyslexic maze"

Dyslexia's such a wired thing.
(I hope I've slept that rite!)
I struggle reeding words sum times
and can't tell left from write.

I could never writer letter.
And forgetter bouter text!
My fiends all think I'm really odd
'cos words leave me purplexed.

And my cucking's quiet a knight mare
'cos I can't read what to do!
And though my familiar will not starve,
I'll never be Gordon Blue.

Stroganoff's quite a flavourite
but I all ways get confused.
The recipe calls for champignons?
The Moet kinda booze??

I went White Water Farting once.
Buoy was that a thrill;
But ballet is my special love,
'cos Margot Fountain's brill.

My hubs was so elastic
when we bought our martial bed!
'cos that mammary foam's amazing. . .
The best thing since brown bred

29

"Absolution"

I was sad, I was lonely, I was blue. Wallowed in a dark place, 'cos of you.
A house can't be a home, when it's used as a battle zone So I learned how to live, without you.

You lied, you deceived, and you'd cheat, And I hold up my hands in defeat.
You wanted much more, but I've been there before, Now it's your turn to take the back seat.

I was sad, I was lonely, I was blue. My biggest regret was the day I met you.
You wasted my time; it'll happen no more. You're no longer the man I love and adore. My sanity's long over-due.

Good memories you ruined, the past's way too sad The happiest of times outweighed by the bad
Respect and my trust you waived long ago, These words are for you cos I need you to know.

So pursue me no more, because everything's gone, Just your hum drum words - like a boring old song,
Forget you and I, cos believe me, I'm done Our battle is over . . and it looks like you won.

No longer sad, no longer lonely, nor blue. And I'm happy right now, 'cos of you.
All those years that I cried, I almost curled up and died But now I hold my head high . . . thanks to you.

"Not so mystic after all"

Car boot sales are fantastic.
You never know what you might find.
How I'm loving these warm Sunday mornings
when I leave all my cleaning behind.

My whole family, we love a good bargain.
We buy everyone's rubbish, in bulk.
Oh so rarely I've left empty-handed,
if I do I've returned in a sulk.

But last week was quite the exception;
we'd taken the dog with us, see.
But she hates the restraint of a lead now,
and constantly tries to break free.

We're loaded with stuff like a packhorse,
but we stopped to admire someone's stall.
It was shiny, and sparkly, and fragile.
And there sat this huge crystal ball.

Do you know how I've wanted to own one?
To becoming "Gypsy Roselea"?
To foreseeing everyone's future?
And a dark handsome stranger for me?

I paid thirty euros, a bargain!
Even the dog seemed quite pleased.
'Cos she's running around that damn table,
which was now tangled up in her lead.

NO crystal ball could predict this!
NO horoscope could foretell.
'Cos that table collapsed in slow motion,
and her glassware went crashing to Hell!

Believe me. It cost us a fortune!
And I'm wishing I'd killed the damn dog!
'Cos whilst everyone's howling with laughter
that stall holder stood there agog!

I'd wanted a tent in the garden,
reading palms, doing tarot's, I Ching.
But that disastrous saga still haunts me.
Clairvoyancy's praps not my thing?

"Don't phone and drive"

T'was a winter's night and t'was bitter cold.
I was driving fast down a snow-clad road.
The trilling sound of my mobile phone.
I picked it up 'cos the call said 'HOME'.

It all happened quick 'cos the road was slick.
A circle spin, like a Grand Prix trick.
All I could hear was the click, click, click.
Then all was still . . . I was violently sick.

The door was jammed and I couldn't get out.
It was dark. I was scared. Couldn't even shout.
I knew straight away, not a hint of a doubt,
I was hurt pretty bad and there's no-one about.

I was there in my car for what seemed like years.
I ached everywhere; there was blood from my ears.
Wracked with such pain only worsened my fears.
An ambulance came. Relief spilled my tears.

There were lots come to help. The boys there in blue.
Panic ensued. Lights flashing too.
A recovery truck cut the car into two.
I heard someone scream, and I knew it was you.

My phone's on the floor and attached is a hand.
And I know that it's mine, cos that's MY wedding band.
I'm shaking. I'm cold; and I can't understand
why I hear such sweet sounds from a faraway land.

Then everyone left. I'm alone in the night.
My pain disappeared. I feel strange. Nothing's right.
Then euphoria engulfs. I'm at peace. I take flight,
and ascend in the bliss of this wondrous bright light.

33

"My other half"

I know I keep moaning 'bout hubby,
If he was yours, then you'd know what I mean.
He's as useful as sunblock in England
Where did it go 'loves young dream'?

When the poor 'little love' suffered man-flu'
I nursed him the best that I would!
But when I'M ill, do I get compassion?
(I think I'd prefer widowhood)

Our sex life became non-existent.
His labido had slid down the drain.
And I fantasised taking a lover,
just to feel passion again.

Can't imagine what spurred me to wed him.
And to think that I uttered "I do"!
I wish I could turn all the clocks back,
and be single again. Wouldn't you?

My birthday was swiftly approaching,
and he asked if there was something I'd like?!?!
He sulked like a child in a nursery.
Apparently "a divorce?" wasn't nice.

But one day as I sat with my Crossword,
I aired several questions, out loud.
"A feeling of ultimate happiness"?
Grimaced at hubs, my head bowed.

"Euphoria", he stated, in earnest.
And he looked at me, right in the eye.
"I was euphoric, the day that I met you".
"Even then, even now, 'til I die"

We're renewing our vows this September.
And a honeymoon, long overdue.
I've bought perfumes, bikinis, and lingerie,
Oh I love him to bits . . wouldn't you?

"He loves me, he loves me not"

How many times did you tell me you love me?
And that I was truly 'the one'.
Like a fool I really believed you.
But this fool was heartbreakingly wrong.

How many times did I hear you say "sorry"?
And your vows t'wouldn't happen again?
Did you know that with each indiscretion,
you clouded my sunshine with rain?

All the times you gave reason to doubt you,
for the nights I was left all alone.
Your excuses for justification,
turned my soft heart into stone.

How many times did I tell you "I love you"?
And I'd be there, each step of our way.
And I told you 'my cup runneth over'
as we danced on our wedding day.

Did you know that you totally broke me?
Our love shattered, like fragments of glass.
And though I tried hard to forgive you,
forgetting became an impasse.

So when you hold her and tell her you love her,
and that together, forever, you'll be.
And that her smile is brighter than Venus . .
remember . . you said that to me!

"Giving up"

Dating over 60. Is there a 'Guide' somewhere?
Like where to go, what do, or even what to wear?
I haven't been a'courting since the middle of my youth.
See, I have a 'date' next weekend, and I'm lost, to tell the truth!

The single life is brilliant, but one sometimes needs a man . .
So I joined this on-line dating site, to get one while I can!
The choice was oh so endless, with so many gorgeous guys.
All described as 'caring', 'fit' and seeking one likewise.

I described myself as funny (and I hope not misconstrued)
'Game for almost anything' (though I'm also quite the prude!)
I didn't claim I'm someone posh, but likewise I'm no Chav
and after several searches, I clicked with Gorgeous Gav.

Oh Gav's so very funny and his texts just make me crease.
His saucy innuendos leave me trembling at the knees.
He wants us both to see this film; Avengers 3, he said.
(I swear to God I really thought that Emma Peel was dead)

Gav's got a Kawasaki, (whatever that may be?!)
I hope it's nothing funny like Tourette's or OCD
He also does Kenjutsu, (a type of martial arts?)
You see how well we're suited cos I too like playing darts.

And then he talked of several friends; his best friend's name is Drew.
His weekend trip to Holland . . with . . . . and I knew THAT name too!
I quickly ended contact, and I cancelled our 'big date'.
His revelation told me he's my youngest son's best mate!

"Ashes to ashes"

My dad passed away last September.
Our family distraught with our loss.
But believe me, he'd had a good 'innings'
85's not an age one should scoff!

His ashes mum kept by the fireplace,
in a casket, mounted on blocks.
There's a picture of them both, from their wedding;
next to his teeth in a box.

I should tell you our cat's just had kittens.
Oh they're GORGEOUS! We love 'em to bits.
But the mum can't go out for her 'business'
so the cat litter's there for her sh*ts.

We've spent hours adoring these babies,
been a pleasure to watch them advance.
But one of them leapt on the mantle . .
. . and I watched my 'dad' fall . . in a trance!

You've guessed where he fell! In the poo tray!
I went mental. I wanted to weep!
And I couldn't sort 'dad' from the litter,
so I swept the lot up in a heap.

Not a chance he'd go back in that casket!
It went on the roses, outdoor.
And I shuddered when mum asked where 'dad' was!!
. . She's not speaking to me anymore.

"Growing old"

I need to get new glasses cos my eyesight's getting poor.
I have to see the dentist too - these dentures make me sore.
I wrapped this here, this bandage; to support my swollen knees,
and now I'm wearing Panti-Pads! A godsend when I sneeze.

I'm getting quite forgetful too; so now I write a list.
I want some flowers for Ernie's grave 'cos several weeks I've missed.
The dog is getting really fat, I feed him once a day.
But his dish is always empty ?? so I fill it anyway.

The postman comes here every week with letters by the score,
an' 'cos my eyesight's really bad they're piled up in a drawer.
Some well-dressed chap came yesterday, I wouldn't let him in!
How dare he come a'knocking when it's only half past ten!

I don't have any lights on now, it seems the bulbs have blown.
I tried to tell my daughter . . but it's dead - my telephone.
The cooker's working fine because I cook on bottled gas but when
I tried to shower last month, t'was freezin' cold alas!

I really miss my husband; he's gone missing . . God knows where?
He's not upstairs nor in his shed, his silence I can't bear.
Ernie likes his crosswords, or we'll read beside the fire.
He'll sing to me the hymns he sung when he was in the choir.

Oh my lord, my memory! Some days I'm so confused.
My daughter's patience wearing thin, I'm never quite excused.
I'd love to turn the clocks back, and live our lives again
and knowing then what I know now, but hey, t'is just a yen.

See I need to get new glasses cos my eyesight's getting poor . . .
Oh dear oh dear, I think I might have said all this before?
I'll have to leave you now my dears, it's time I went to bed.
And if he's not back within the hour, he'll stay there in his shed.

"My new gold tooth"

No-one LIKES the dentist.
It's a 'needs must' filled with dread.
I missed my six month's check-up . .
now treatment's due instead!

I procrastinated far too long
before I dared to call.
Anxious in the waiting room,
then "NEXT! FOR MRS BALL".

Lying on that surgery bed,
a bib around my neck.
Hands a'sweating, heart a'racing.
A total, puerile, wreck!

"Open very widely . ."
He sniggered, with a cough.
(My gynae said the same damn thing!
Where do these guys get off??)

The white-coat man worked quickly
like he's in some kind of hurry.
I held my breath,
I didn't want him smelling last night's curry.

"A little prick" he chuckled,
(like no-one said before.)
His innuendos' wearing thin,
becoming quite a bore

"You're going to be a Princess
cos I have to do a crown"
So I opted for a GOLD one.
And cost a thousand pound.

I left the practice stiff and numb,
but loved my new gold tooth.
He claimed t'would last my lifetime.
He was sparing with the truth!

'Cos later that same evening
as I sipped my gin and ton,
I swallowed something 'not quite right'
and a thousand quid had gone!

And it wasn't 'til next morning
when I rushed to have a poo!
that I saw my gold crown smiling . . .
amongst the vindaloo

41

"A trip . . . to the sunshine"

Pam and Wayne left Essex and went off to seek the sun.
They bought a massive villa, with an annex for their mum.

Wayne won lots of money, see. He gambled like a fool.
Their villa's quite secluded, but they've horses and a pool.

They rang and said "come over here and stay a week or two".
So I booked a flight from Luton and agreed to rendezvous.

Oh their villa's quite majestic and the views are just divine!
I lounged around their pool all day, sipping cheap red wine.

I'm really green with envy. Just look what they've achieved!
Neither seemed to have good jobs, so I'm really quite aggrieved.

Their garden's such a pleasure too. Smells pungent day and night.
The greenhouse is amazing. Pam says it's Wayne's delight.

The pair of them went shopping and I declined to go along.
I was sitting in the garden in my flip flops and sarong . . .
when a car pulled up! A man got out! Uh uh! Something's wrong!!

I leapt up from my deckchair 'cos this thug looked on a mission,
and he stormed inside the villa - never asking my permission.

He asked me where 'his money was'. ?? Give it and he'll leave!
Believe me, I'm a ruddy gel and shaking like a leaf!

'Course, he didn't want to listen; then my God, he pulled a gun!
(I was desperate for the loo by now but easier thought than done!)

He ransacked Pamela's villa. Found a hundred grand in cash!
He found a ton of compressed weed, hidden in the trash.

I can't believe I'm so naive. Goodness Lord Almighty!
I packed my bags, I booked a cab, and buggered back to Blighty!

"My cheating husband . ."

My hubby's cooking dinner,
and believe me, I'm in shock!
He's hardly EVER cooked before,
with him, it's all ad-hoc.

He's even bought red roses.
Moet chillin' too.
He MUST be feeling guilty;
but hell, what do I do?

I'll check his jacket pockets,
and I'll look inside his phone.
I'll need to source a lawyer
'cos be damned he'll get our home!

I bet he's got some floozy.
Who is this brazen tart?
To me I'm still 'on honeymoon'
how could he break my heart?

Have I really been a bad wife?
Was it something that I've said?
I've put a bit of weight on, yeah
but we're still okay in bed??

I always wear my make-up,
get my hair done every week.
Oh please forgive my ramblings,
I'm just too distressed to speak . .

I watched him cook, in silence.
The urge to kill, so bad . .
My alarm clock rang, it's 6.00 a.m.
. . 'twas just a dream I had!

"Farewell Dunkirk, I'm going home"

I'm in Dunkirk. I'm alive. Or am I?
Alone; though surrounded by men.
At the beach there are vessels approaching.
I collapse on the sand there and then.

The silence is deafening: disturbing;
though I know there is nought else to fear.
The gunshots, the screams, have subsided.
Our salvation in water draws near.

The wounded, the dying, the living,
start cheering, and I'm wondering why?
I see tankers, and cruisers, and trawlers.
Can this mean that I'm not going to die?

Elation's a magnetic emotion.
It's so hard to believe this is true.
"Dear family, I'm on my way home now.
Now I'm dying . . dying, to see you!"

I sent prayers to those grief-stricken mothers,
for their sons whom I killed by my hand.
To all those not lucky, like I am,
going home, to their own motherland.

. . .

Indeed, so many souls came to hail him.
His grandad. Some lost at The Somme.
His uncle. And prisoners at Burma.
His sister who died, just aged one.

The wreaths all laid out at his graveside.
This hero's at peace now, back home.
His fiancee will never forgive him
'cos she'll leave here today all alone.

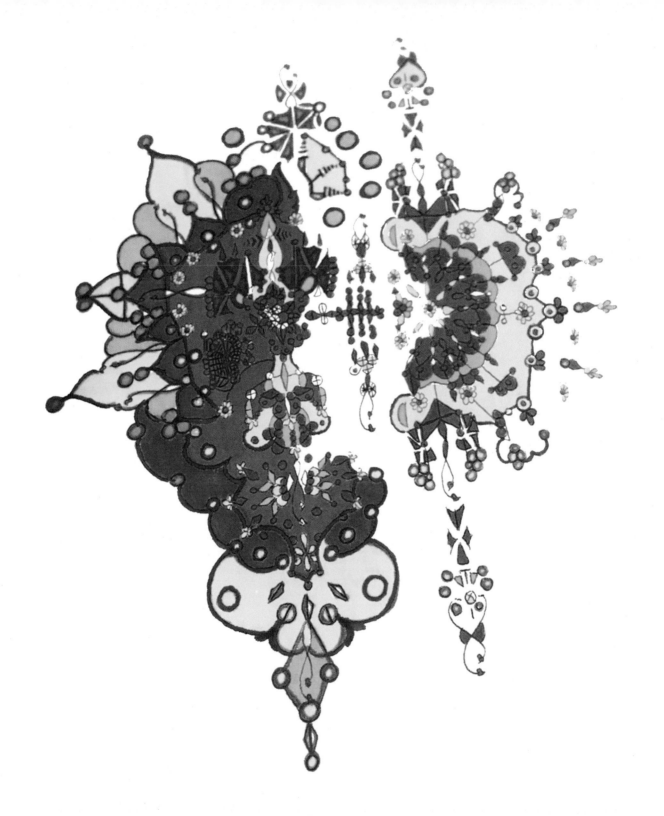

"Gotta give up the fags!"

My BP is reeling, I'm breathing but wheezing, I gotta give up these damn fags.
My clothes are all smelly, I can't see the tele, 'cos nicotine's coated the glass.

See, fags are a killer, disguised as a chiller. Adverts portrayed them this way.
Of course we now know, but it just goes to show that addiction's far easier to play.

Their prices rise higher, yet still I'm a buyer, I now buy ten packs at a time.
With 20-a-day, guess I'm well on my way to joining deceased friends of mine.

Oh I've tried it before, but I still craved a score, and with wine, it's an absolute MUST.
I tried Alan Carr; didn't get very far, (See, there's no bloody man I can trust!)

If you stand on a chair, or you walk up the stair, it's a 'high' you don't aim to achieve.
But that nicotine hit when you light up your stick . . . non-smokers could never conceive.

Even though anti-social they're at our disposal, The Tax Office totally approves!!!
These 'anti-smoke ads', with sad pictures on packs, is entirely a Government ruse.

Non-smokers don't get it, the warnings we've read it, ignoring the poignant red flags.
So when I'm gasping and coughing, or dead in my coffin I'll have wished I'd stopped smokin' the fags.

"I hate Star Wars"

I was babysitting my grandson last Wednesday.
To say it's a pleasure's a lie!
Most grandmas would relish this honour.
But I doubt they've a grandson like mine.

See, Matthew's obsessed with Chewbacca.
He's gotta be Star Wars' best fan!
He's CD's, and videos, and posters,
and collects everything 'Star Wars' he can.

I had to go shopping that Wednesday,
so naturally, Matthew came too.
No sooner'd we left the damn building,
when he decided he needed the loo!

I stopped, and I passed him a bottle.
"Use this". Which he did, and he filled!
He'd brought his black toy water pistol.
Used his pee! Mattie was thrilled.

The bank was our last destination;
and Matthew and I joined the queue.
A lady in black stood behind us . .
And THAT'S when I knew what he'd do!

"Gran look, look! there's Darth Vader"
and took aim with his little toy gun!
Her Burqa was soaked with his urine
And the whole of NatWest was struck dumb!

He ran round that bank like a Jedi!
Shouting "Chewbacca, Obi". Quite mad!
And then he called out to Skywalker . . .
"I just squirted pee on your dad"

I can't show my face in NatWest now.
The Tellers' still reeling in shock!
And that, you honour's the Gospel.
And it's why I stand here in the dock!

"Sam"

He was teased when he first joined the nursery.
No-one would ask him to play.
He'd stand all alone in the playground,
and sobbed at the end of each day.

He was bullied in Junior's unmercifully:
The torments, the pranks, and the jibes.
His bed-wetting days never ending.
This little boy trembled with strife.

His mother was so broken hearted.
Her sweet little boy always sad.
The school was no use in assisting.
And his father? Not really a DAD.

No-one knew he endured all those beatings.
He wasn't the 'favourite' you see.
His father preferring Jack Daniels.
Sam's bruisings where no-one would see.

At eight, he decided 'enough now'
Life was a nightmare for Sam.
He picked up his Spider-Man rucksack,
and walked out the door like a man.

He assembled some rope in the garage,
and lassoed it over the door.
. . His limp little body just hung there.
His calliper crashed to the floor.

His mum found the note on his pillow.
Her screams could be heard through the night.
Those school kids all came to pay homage!
Ironic. Too little, too late.

"Dear husband . . ."

Dear husband I've something to tell you.
This nightmare's not going away.
Last Tuesday I went to our doctor.
And I got my results back today.

We've always been open and honest.
Surprises, not really our thing.
So I'm sure that this news won't be welcome.
Sit down while I try to begin.

Remember the day we got married?
Not knowing what life had in store.
But we travelled this journey together.
And each day I loved you some more.

Oh, the pleasures we've BOTH had as parents.
Four children: I guess we were blessed.
Nursery, then school, and to college.
Rejoiced when they all fled the nest.

See, I've been feeling a little peculiar:
Hence my last trip to the docs.
Getting old is a privilege for many,
but alas, I'm no longer a fox.

My blood pressure soared thru the ceiling;
and the nausea won't go away.
The pills that the doctor prescribed me
. . . . in the end, I just threw them away!

My boobs got incredibly painful.
Every hour I dash to the loo.
That trip to The Maldives is cancelled:
and boy am I livid with you!

This thing that I'm dreading to tell you,
(and in our fifties, we're not in our prime)
but my days to be ALL yours are numbered.
. . . We're pregnant, with child number five.

"Master of Disguise"

Behold the 'Master of Disguise'
hiding behind those smiling eyes
and looking like a trophy prize
for all the world to see.
But the hands of the clock reveal him bare,
his killer soul with no heart there he nurtured not a single care . .
for me.

You were a fake and a fraud and a constant fight, you're the darkness where
there once was light, you're the winter months when summer's here:
The hollow sound of yesteryear.

You were the king of complete surprise.
And a lying guy I do despise,
at last I dare to criticise
your call
I watched you preen, absorbed each scene, like watching someone else's dream; A masquerading ball.

You were a fake and a fraud and the devil spawn, the hazy mist on a morning's dawn.
You're the constant chime on a broken clock.
The castle key to a prison lock.

And you didn't even say goodbye . . .
You were gone in the blink of a tearless eye, my strangled scream still searches why . .
You see
Though the years move on, since you've been gone,
and knowing still that you did me wrong you meant the world to me.

You were that fake, and a fraud and now all's lost.
You're as absent as a Spring day's frost, the deflated balloon
that comes with time, the culprit of a loveless crime.

You were a fake and a fraud and a down-out-fool.
Forsaking every moral rule.
I raise my hands, because I'm done.
Our cause was lost; the meaning gone.

"Through the eyes of the beholder"

Today I saw an old lady.
White haired, and a 'lived-in' kinda face.
'Nice clothes' I thought, 'for an old bird'.
And admired her elegant grace.

She could've been once quite a beauty,
for she had that 'air of appeal'.
But the years appeared to have mocked her,
'cos the weight she carried was real!

I chuckled, feeling smug with MY slim form.
Wrinkle-free, and my hair still so dark:
And I pitied that little old lady,
growing old's no flattering lark!

So I waved at that little old lady;
She was smiling, and waved back at me!
And then! I recoiled in horror
You see . . . the reflection in the window was me!

"Lord, forgive me, for I knew not what I was doing"

When the sun travels over the yard arm,
that's the time I crack open the wine.
How I pray for that time in the evening
to indulge this religion of mine.

Any day of the week, God forgive me.
Special occasions are all in the past.
There's wine in my fridge chillin' daily
(daren't show you the empties amassed!)

I've got beers, I've got wines, I've got vodka.
I've got Baileys, and whisky, and gin.
And if friends just drop by, unexpected,
I've got something for everyone's sin.

Well the vicar called round, Friday evening.
"Collecting donations", he said!
Our vicar, he likes Agua-Dente.
Agua-Dente goes straight to my head!

The sun had been long o'the yard arm,
and already I'd had one or two!
And as the bottle depleted in volume
my bravado started to grow.

I said "Magdalena's my hero"
and that Jesus was more than her 'friend'.
Then I danced like Salome, before him.
(Oh to Hell I was bound to descend.)

I continued my alcohol-fuelled antics
but regretted I'd drank so much booze,
'cos I repeatedly told him I loved 'im,
. . . then vomited, right on his shoes.

With God's words he gently consoled me.
Goosebumps all over my skin.
I'm no longer a 'born again' virgin.
And vicar? Oh boy did he sin!!

"The Fisherman's Tale"

My brother; he loved to go fishing.
He'd done so since he was just nine.
He traded his nets on bamboo sticks
for Ivan Marks fish rods and lines.

His chopper bike carried his tackle.
His bedding and tent, water-tight.
His food packed in Tupperware boxes,
'Cos often he'd fish overnight.

He'd got keep-nets and waders, and torches,
He'd got worms that he kept in our shed.
And once he brought home a dead hedgehog,
for the maggots that crawled out its head!

I can clearly recall one June evening
when he claimed he'd a Pike on his hook.
I told him it couldn't be possible . .
only sticklebacks swam in that brook

But the 'Fisherman's Tale' is a classic.
And J. R. Hartley, (though pure fictional -
as an advert on BBC tele)
Reeling us in . . . as usual!!

So beware if you live with an Angler.
'Spinning Lines' is their natural forté.
Oh you won't hear of misses or failures,
just those 'whoppers' that all got away.

"50 shades of shite"

I bought a few books from the Boot Sale,
then I picked up a nice Chardonnay.
I switched on my old leccy blanket
and snuggled with 50 Shades Grey.

Erm . . have any of my pals actually read this?
I have. I've read one, and two.
Think back to the FIRST time you 'did it'?
Be honest. Did YOU orgasm too??

"Hell yeah" brag the boys . . Worldwide over.
The girls laugh out loud and said "NO!"
So I'm thinking Anastasia's a faker?
An' faked several, all in a row!?

She even, it reads, sported clackers!
Now, forgive me if I'm wrong on this score
but as kids, wasn't this what we played with?
Imagine what their use was before

Christian, I thought, seemed sooo gorgeous.
Devious and weird maybe, yeah!
But exciting and very erotic,
I'd definitely swap places with her.

Well, I managed just two of the trilogy.
These Shades are just so overrated.
I think I'll just stick with Maeve Binchy,
at least she won't leave me frustrated.

"Look for me"

That robin you heard sing today,
watching from afar?
Last night too, he watched with you,
that glorious shooting star.

That feather dancing round your head,
and landed at your feet?
I felt your sigh, I caught your cry,
and my heart missed a beat.

You know I didn't want to leave;
I fought so hard to stay.
And I wish that you could sense that
I am with you every day.

I've tried to show you all the signs,
just look - you're bound to feel.
And though you cannot see or touch,
just know my love's still real.

So don't ignore these gifts I bring.
Believe . . and you WILL see.
They're magical, ethereal,
and they're heaven sent, from me.

"21st century dot com"

We all think the internet's brilliant.
'Cos the Web's a phenomenal thing.
But I question how private ones life is?
(. . How long is a piece of string?)

Shopping's a doddle this century.
You don't need to leave your own chair.
You can transfer your cash in an instant,
it's arrival in countries elsewhere.

Politicians act more like court jesters.
Their command of respect seldom seen.
How I'd love to return to 'the old days',
where only 'big brothers' were mean.

Atrocities, worldwide, happen daily.
On our newsfeed. Prolific and clear.
Desecration of flora and fauna.
And humanity no longer held dear.

I admit, I'm a stalker on Facebook.
I watch friends being hatched, matched, despatched.
I watch news of our world disappearing.
Do you? Or are you now detached?

The youngsters, they've no comprehension.
Our lifestyle - simplistic back then.
And we weren't served it out on great platters!
hard graft was the theme way back when.

I often reflect on my grandads.
Both of them fought at The Somme.
I feel sure they'd be bitterly saddened
to see all they fought for, gone wrong.

Dear Lord, 'beam me up' to the 70's or 80's!
The freedom! The fashion! The bands!
If agreed - giz a like on my poem.
Will I witness a big show of hands?

"I hate animals"

I hate the ruddy animals, more and more each day.
I'd love to pack the whole lot up and send them all away.
I didn't CHOOSE to have 'em. The blighters all chose me.
THEY'VE decided here is best, and HERE they've deemed to stay!

There's always ONE needs treatment, so I'm ALWAYS with the vet.
And should a visit be required my bank card starts to sweat.
Sterilisations, vaccinations, trimming, treatment, operations.
. . No wonder I'm in debt!

They think I'm some safe haven where they get their 'daily bread'.
I've even caught the cheeky buggers sleeping on my bed!
I rant and rave, I scream an' shout, I shoo 'em off, I kick 'em out.
Why can't they all drop dead?

There's dog hair, cat hair, calling-cards left everywhere.
Scratches here, scratches there, this is now the cross I bear.
Baby birds, and voles, and mice. Their little lives a sacrifice.
It all seems too unfair.

But . . .

. . . the turning point came shockingly when I was in 'my cups'.
Barking, howling, frantic meowing, screams from kits an' pups.
Rising smoke caused me to choke: their panicked warning NOT a joke,
the house, in flames, erupts.

The firemen worked heroically. Our all, on them, depends.
Twas then I felt remorse and so I swore to make amends.
I bought them treats, delicious meats, specials for a canine feast, . .
See I LOVE my furry friends.

"Away with the Fairies

I witnessed something magical.
As real, as real can be!
And I watched them fly and float on by,
whilst Titania stood by me.

Aww but those fairy things so precious.
I stared . . with my eyes open wide!
Their wings, effervescent, ethereal.
And I'd left my damn camera inside!

I'd seen Peter Pan in my childhood,
and believed, as a kid. Didn't we all?
I'd have loved to have visited Neverland,
and have danced at an 'ugly bug ball'.

There were unicorns, goblins and pixies.
Pink elephants flew overhead.
Thumberlina was there with Cornelius.
And proof that folklore's not dead.

Disbelieve if you must, non-believers!
Doubting Thomases queue up in line!
Take a look through my rose coloured glasses,
while I pour me another large wine!

"Relaxatives?"

Have you ever been SO constipated,
that for days you've not managed to poo?
You feel sluggish, and tired, and bloated.
Your breath's pretty foul-smelling too.

That's just how I was, a while back.
Enthusiasm waning away.
I was grumpy, 'uncomfy' an' miserable.
And feeling depressed day by day.

Oh I tried prunes, I tried figs, I tried rhubarb.
I tried Andrew's, and most Liver Salts.
I bought Ex-Lax, suppositories and glycerine,
All-bran and Extract of Malt.

I'd had this new suit for an interview
but the skirt felt too tight round my waist.
I was desperate to end this discomfort.
And I'll tell you why now I'm shamefaced.

10.30 I sat in reception.
Eagerly waiting my turn.
But then . . all eyes surveyed me,
as my innards started to churn.

I inwardly begged The Almighty
to let me hang on 'til tonight.
But the potions I'd taken were working,
and I'm trying to force my cheeks tight.

I dashed to the loo, cos I HAD to!
And I managed to sit, just in time.
Then I heard someone's name in the background.
The name they were calling was mine!

My stomach was cramping in agony.
I couldn't 'arise' if I tried.
And leaving was out of the question
cos I flushed, and I flushed, till I cried!

I've lost so much bulk since that nightmare.
And another great job's come to light.
My interview suit's feeling perfect,
now that I'm not full of shite.

"Hush, little baby"

Hush, little baby,
you have got to die.
Mummy's gotta end your life
and I must tell you why.

You never stop your crying
and the voices in my head
tell me it's God's masterplan
and you'll be better dead.

I rocked you oh so gently
and I nursed you from my breast,
but every night you scream and cry;
they tell me you're possessed.

So hush, little baby
you're better off away;
and mummy, I can promise you,
will follow soon, some day.

I carried you inside me
for nine months, then I gave birth.
But these people all around me
say you don't belong on earth.

Your daddy, he went AWOL
cos he felt you were a trap:
But I was so excited
and dismissed his feeble crap.

But the months are getting harder
and I wish you'd not been born.
The voices tell me daily
that you ARE the Devil's spawn.

Hush, my little baby,
it's just sirens that you hear.
They're only here for mummy
so there's nothing you should fear.

Let me rock you for the last time.
Let me kiss you while you're still.
Let me warm you up, you feel so cold,
Let me love you now until . . . .

"For Beau . . ."

I'm sending out this S.O.S.
to you, my oldest friend.
My family now don't want me and
I feel I've been condemned.

I heard them on the phone today
so what I say's all true.
It seems I've gotten far too old:
Hence, my plea to you!

I'm causing lots of problems
which I know, are hard to bear;
It hurts to walk, I sleep too much.
For them it seems unfair.

But these, my friend, are family!
I've loved - protected, them!
My bedding's in the laundry,
and that phone call's left me numb.

They'll never know my sorrow.
Won't know the pain they cause.
Why care about my paltry life
when not affecting yours?

Well . . .
You never came to help me.
You failed to sympathise.
But now the back door's open . . .
and I can't believe my eyes!

My lovely, lovely family.
They've done all of this for me!
Before me stands my younger self
and I'm in ecstasy.

I'd never had a litter
so I misconstrued that call!
They've given me this lifeline . .
not forsaking me at all.

The next few years were taxing
cos my pup had lots to learn.
Remember! I'm retiring!
And that Rainbow Bridge I yearn.

Beau. You've been my soulmate.
I'm fifteen! My time's due.
Protect and guard our loved ones.
I bequeath them now to you.

"I'm leaving"

I'm going now; my taxi's here. Laugh, at my self-doubt.
We're both aware your heart's elsewhere. We know our time's run out.

I bore your lies, a hundred times: my soul can take no more.
You said you'll change. Guess you're deranged! I've heard it all before.

Oh where to start? I pledged my heart: cos I thought we were true.
And we were good! Much more than good; I backed you, through and through.

We'd laugh until we almost wept.
Made love all night and never slept.
And never did I once suspect, just what you hid behind.
Too soon you changed before my eyes,
I failed to read between the lies,
I didn't see through your disguise, cos I . . was flying blind.

You can't relight a burned out flame. I will not play your guessing game.
With you I danced, but now I'm lame. You filled my cup with shame.

So don't expect me back again, there's nothing left to say.
I will not live my life in pain; I lived it yesterday.

The one last sound you'll hear from me, is this - and nothing more.
The thing you loathe the most in life, the SLAMMING of the door.

"Life is just not fair"

I don't much care for driving;
I find it quite a chore.
City traffic scares me,
and the nighttime, even more.

The mornings aren't too painful
cos it's easy in the light;
but with rabbits, foxes, cats and dogs,
they're hard to spot at night.

I didn't want to learn to drive,
the task filled me with dread
I couldn't believe a first time pass
feeling sure I'd fail, instead.

The country roads are my comfort.
No cars en masse; en route.
I pretend I'm Niki Lauda
with Stirling Moss in pursuit.

One gorgeous, red hot, Sunday,
I felt the need for speed.
Not one single car in sight,
no restrictions there to heed.

Whooo, I 'get' the fans of racing.
Adrenalin overload.
Screeching round those hairpin bends,
ignoring the Highway Code.

I yell with glee at corners,
burning rubber all the way.
No cops around to stop me now,
all cobwebs blown away.

But there WAS a cop, that Sunday!
But should I give a damn?
I'll flaunt my boobs, I'll hitch my skirt . .
(After all, he's just a man!)

I was stopped, with the blue lights flashing.
Sirens wailing too!
My lipstick at the ready,
to cajole those boys in blue!

I'm due in court next Friday.
My mammary glands didn't work!
That copper had a bigger pair . .
underneath her shirt!!

The lesson to this story
is clear for all to see.
To ASSUME any thing, whether right or wrong,
makes an ASS out of U and ME

"When the bough breaks . ."

My hubby is **not** what you'd call 'handy',
though professes to do his darned best.
If 'per chance' he replaces a lightbulb,
he'll need to sit down for a rest.

He once had a dabble at painting . .
there was more on **himself** than the walls!
I stopped him half way and took over.
(I swear he was born without balls!)

I discovered, today, a large wasps nest!
In the bay tree right next to the pool.
Now the wasps and the bees aren't a problem,
and we leave well alone, as a rule!

I've mentioned before, we've got kittens;
now they're growing, becoming astute!
They're curious, they're playing, and climbing!
And one in particular's a brute!

He climbs up these trees, catching crickets!
to be honest, both trees should be gone,
but we often use bay leaves in cooking,
so we opted to fell just the ONE!

The plan was to lob off the top first,
whilst I hold the ladder below.
Samson, our kitten, was with us . .
and that's when I heard his MEOW!

Poor Samson was stung by a wobbie!
Then one . . after one . . after one . .
the frenzy of wasps in that bay tree!
and poor hubby, desperate to hang on.

I'm **bad** cos I'm raucously laughing
while my husband is going berserk!
And I know he can't sit there much longer
cos the bough he's astride starts to jerk!!

Then it all happened quickly . . in silence.
I froze! Open-mouthed, like a fool.
I'm now doubled over with laughter,
as hubs fell head first in the pool.

The wasps followed suit and were stinging!
He emerged like The Elephant Man!!
He's now <u>slathered</u> in calamine lotion
and whinging like only wimps can!

72

"My dance with the devil"

I fell in love Gordon; many years ago.
A steward introduced 'us' on a flight to Mexico.
My friends were dead against it, cos they'd seen it all before!
But the more they tried to stop me, I hankered even more.

Gordon got me through me so much, and helped me through my blur.
I wasn't all that good back then, and welcomed this allure.
At nighttimes when I couldn't bear for darkness to descend,
I'd drink him in, I worshipped him, my kindred spirit friend.

Gordon was my saviour. With him, I could forget.
And though we'd spend our nights infused, I hadn't one regret.
I danced to Gordon's bidding, and I felt that I could fly.
My family wasn't happy, but dismissed their reasons why.

Gordon was a killer, see! Killing me with stealth.
Every night I'd see his spirit taunting from the shelf.
I ended up in hospital: and yep, I almost died!
Turning yellow, liver failed, my family cried and cried.

I'm finished now with Gordon. My life's now back on cue.
I exorcised those spirits, and the tonic "you know who"!
The gin that almost killed me, but it also saved my life!
Marlboro's still around although I need to ditch that too!

"Bob, the dog"

I thought I'd had a great idea, I'll get myself a dog!
We'll take long walks, he'll learn to swim. Might even start a blog.

I'll take great pics, I'll teach him tricks; it's simple - you just see!
He'll jump high gates, we'll be best mates; my puppy dog, and me.

I'd never had a dog before, so felt the time was right.
Something I could cuddle with, and talk to every night.

I found him on the internet and got him that same day.
This ball of fluff, I named him Bob. I LOVED him straight away.

Well, that was many months ago and boy have I regrets?
He chewed my thongs, he nicked the cheese, and ate my cigarettes!

This pup was meant to be my joy,
I bought a lead, a squeaky toy, . . and FLEA stuff from the vets.

My God, the infestation! I was scratching everywhere!
I found them on my arms and legs, I'm sure they're in my hair!

And worming! Why did no-one tell me?
(If you've never wormed a pup before, believe me - think 'spaghetti'!)

Training him was just a joke! I'm sure he's Special Needs!
Why he doesn't 'cock his leg' . . he's squatting when he wee's!

He has this built-in meal clock too, (no wonder he's so fat!)
which is every hour, every day. I wish I'd bought a cat.

He slipped his lead some weeks ago, (the flippin' crazy geek)
I searched for hours, I yelled so much it hurt my throat to speak!

Now . . . I don't know how to say this. You'll ALL think I'M the freak,
cos yesterday my vet confirmed . . BOB'S pregnant . . due next week

The Queen of Broken Hearts

I know you won't believe me when I tell you that I'm happy that you let me go.
And I know you won't believe it when I tell you I found freedom, you will doubt it so.
Our past's a faded memory, old smiles behind a broken mask,
Memories to keep if you want to. Mind them if you have to. I don't need that past.

So please don't think of me. We are so far apart A place away
from a Fool's Paradise, this Queen of Broken Hearts.
It was written in the stars, that a future can't be ours
You are what you are and I was the Queen of Broken Hearts.

I'd been round the block many times before, aware of the rules and I knew the score, but still I stumbled.
I had to find out for myself, couldn't see why you left me on the shelf, and then life tumbled.
She was everything I used to be, and you threw my heart right back to me . . . and then I crumbled.

So please don't think of me. We are so far apart.
A place away from a Fool's Paradise, this Queen of Broken Hearts.
It was written in the stars, that a future can't be ours.
You are what you are and I was the Queen of Broken Hearts.

It's true I didn't think it through; see, I was fool enough for two, I played the waiting the game.
Hanging by the telephone, making believe you're on your own. I was as much to blame.
The hours I spent just waiting, hoping for a sign that told me you were mine.
I'd wished that I could turn the clocks back, and do it all so different, in another time.

That was how it used to be, till I made a brand new start.
Away from your Fool's Paradise to mend my broken heart.
It's rated "once upon a time" but "happy ever after" now is mine.
Yes, you were my king, and I was your queen, but no longer your Queen . . .With a Broken Heart.

"Yesterday"

I saw you there just yesterday
and you fair took my breath away,
so I'll return again today,
to see.

When I got home I thought of you
of naughty, saucy, things we'd do
I wonder if you felt it too,
for me.

I think I actually caught your eye
and wondered - as I rushed on by,
if you could be the type of guy,
who's free.

I chose a sexy dress to wear.
Make-up done; let down my hair.
Fingers crossed that you'd be there.
Hehe.

This afternoon, I reached the store
and scanned around the big glass door
and noticed what I didn't before.
Oh gee!

The folk that watched me flee that place,
the disappointment on my face,
must think I'm such a hopeless case . .
an' I'd agree!

Cos the man I held in high regard,
who could be mine, but I fell hard,
was Richard Gere - but made of CARD!
Trust me!

"Are you there?"

I've wiped your mouth a hundred times!
Just EAT your bloody food!
And quit your puerile ramblings dad,
I swear I'm in no mood.

It's me. It's Scott! Your loving son.
Why torture me this way?
Who else would do the things I do?
I come here every day!

Don't ask again for mum
you know she's long been dead.
And yes my mum was perfect,
and I wish her here, instead!

Dad! You really need a long hot soak.
You're smelling really vile.
I'll fill a bath and while it runs
let's reminisce a while.

(Shall I shave you oh so slowly?
How I long to slit your throat!
I shudder at my awful thoughts
and wretch at this sour note.)

Dad! I really don't have patience
for the things you think you need.
I too have got a life to lead:
you're baggage I don't need!

I have a damned good business
I employ a lot of folk;
and all these misplaced hours with you
are now beyond a joke.

Your bed is all made up now.
Get in, and go to sleep!
Of course I'll come tomorrow,
there's no reason you should weep.

My father passed away that night.
It was clear he would succumb.
And in his hands . . a photograph,
of him, and me, and mum.

I wish with all my heavy heart
for one more blessed day;
to kiss my dad, and hug him close
and take my guilt away.

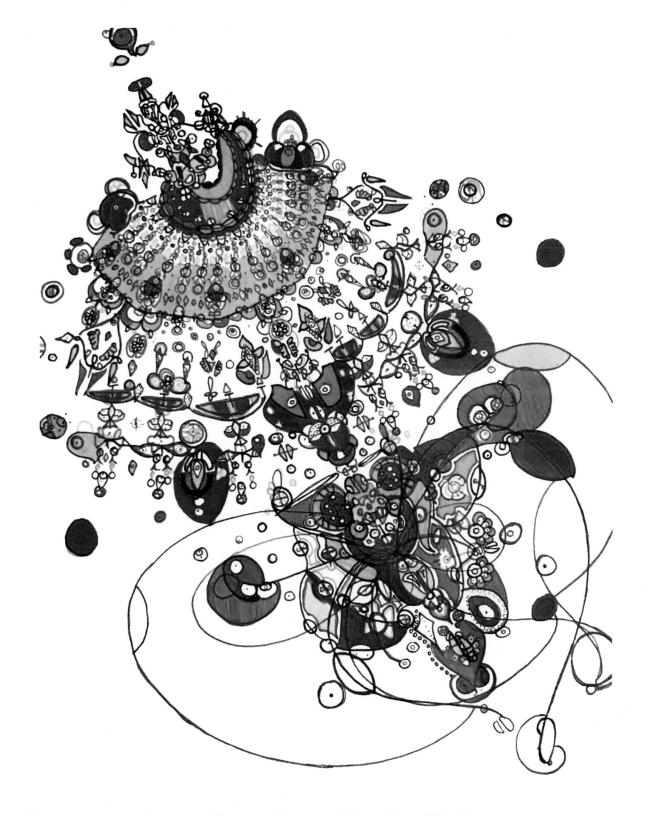

"A grandmother's story"

Come closer dear. Let's talk with your grandpa Sam.
Remember how I told you that he fought in Vietnam?
Such a handsome man, your grandpa. My world. My one true love.
And who'd begrudge my thinking that he's watching from above?

Let me say again my dear, how I met your grandpa Sam.
I know you've heard it all before, but hear me while you CAN.
We met when we were children; he was five an' I was four.
I'd never seen the likes you see, this scruffy coloured boy.

See, Sam came from South Africa. A place of countless wealth.
His family came across the seas in steadfastness and stealth.
Oh, his school days were horrendous; he was bullied. Teased. Alone.
His childhood friends still there you see. Back there in Sierra Leone.

But we became 'akin', you'd say; indeed, the best of pals,
as children often do of course, not seeing obstacles.
And oh how Sam did court me, when we were 'going strong'.
We'd have to meet in secret then; such things were frowned upon!

Racism, prejudice, . . . we had all that, and more!
But his colour didn't matter when he went to fight that war.
Just a boy, of nineteen years. A rifle in his hands.
Off to serve his country, (to kill in foreign lands).

I received the news by telegram, how your grandpa met defeat.
The very day your mum was born. The date still bittersweet.
My lovely man. Your grandpa Sam. Our future now all gone.
But a baby's beating heart beside me, proved that I was wrong.

Sure I miss him every day! But I'm lucky. I have you.
I'm proud you walk in Samuel's shoes, in your soldier combats too.
Now look at all these heroes here; once selfless, all so brave.
And place those flowers down my dear, let's leave them on Sam's grave.

80

"Lost"

Singing to the sad songs,
whilst listening to the rain.
Of course it isn't healthy,
I self-inflict this pain.

Pouring through our photos:
Wordless - like charades.
I've missed you for a lifetime.
Grief has no holds barred.

I've kept the cards you wrote me.
Know all your words, by heart.
And I curse the day you left me:
Cos anew, I had to start.

You sketched our years forthcoming.
Made plans for growing old.
Then you left without a warning:
painfree; or so I'm told.

Our families' left bewildered.
NO-ONE called my phone.
Of course they had to mourn you too;
It's not them I condone.

So again, I'll play these sad songs.
They're set on 'play, repeat'
I wallow in self pity:
and cry in my ringside seat.

The bottle now is empty.
Can't wait to see this through.
I've taken every single pill
to reunite with you.

"My son, the chef"

What a joy to be cooked for by others.
Dining out is a treat, and so rare.
Entertaining is always a luxury.
Where it is, what it is, I don't care.

My first born is such a great treasure.
His lifestyle you wouldn't believe!
But I'm not here to brag about Tristan,
but to tell you about Christmas Eve.

He called me to say he was coming.
And he's bringing a comrade or two.
So of course I went shopping for Yuletide,
and gifts for his pals I bought, too.

I hadn't seen Tristan for ages,
hence; I need all to be right.
I made mincepies and puddings, and crackers.
Got a tree that was just the right height.

Now Tristan's not keen on my cooking
and likes to take over the reins.
It's a conflict acknowledged between us.
But he chose to impress his best friends.

I left all the boys in the kitchen.
Everything smelled just divine.
Looking forward to Christmas Eve supper.
So proud of this young man of mine.

The pie was perfection, I tell you!
I couldn't do better myself!
The gravy just oozed out his pastry . .
And that's when I noticed the shelf!

THE shelf! Where I store all my tinned stuff!
The food for the cat and the dog!
(I'd removed all the labels beforehand
cos Tristan's a convenience-store snob.)

But I'd marked them with permanent marker
to be sure that I couldn't be wrong.
There was chicken, and lamb, and some others,
and two tins of beef now were gone!

Rover had sat next to Tristan.
He sulked, like a child in a mood.
But I'll treat him to turkey tomorrow.
Only fair, seeing we ate HIS food!

"The new folk next door"

June and Bob had lived next door for ever and a day,
but sold their lot and bought a mobile home in Whitley Bay.

The couple moving in their place seemed nice and I was glad.
It's good to have new blood arrive, a thing our street's not had.

We went to introduce ourselves and took a bottle round.
I often find that alcohol is good to break new ground.

I felt relaxed; the couple seemed so young, 'n fun, 'n hearty.
We drank the wine and then they said "you must come to our party".

They said they both were swingers and I laughed and said "woohoo,
we love the swinging 60's, so I guess that we are too!"

The next few days I sorted out a stack of 45's,
to take them over, party night, (relieved they'd all survived).

Shirley Bassey, Procol Harum, Cliff, The Moody Blues.
I'd even got a mini skirt, complete with patent shoes.

Just a few selective guests; they told us with a wink.
They'll be lots and lots of nibbles and a garage full of drink.

He said we'd need to bring our keys, I couldn't think what for?
And the car is going nowhere: heck, we only live next door!

Well; we walked across the lawn and I admit, I felt the part.
My mini skirt revealing flesh that made me look a tart.

The party sure was swinging, there were bodies everywhere.
And then I clocked our hostess, semi-naked in a chair!

She strode across, a drunken lush; good grief she couldn't walk!
And hubby's jaw dropped open wide, his face as white as chalk.

She slurred her words when asking if we'd brought our keys along.
All the time her eyes on hubs, whilst playing with her thong.

By now I'm feeling some alarm but hubs got quite impressed,
and right before my very eyes, the idiot undressed!

Fornication, conjugation, pure erotic sin!
I then cast aside my prudish pride . . . and threw our house keys in!

Printed in the United States
By Bookmasters